AMERICAN DEMOCRACY IN ACTION

How Does Congress Work?

Cathleen Small

LUCENT
PRESS

Published in 2019 by
Lucent Press, an Imprint of Greenhaven Publishing, LLC
353 3rd Avenue
Suite 255
New York, NY 10010

Produced for Lucent by Calcium Creative Ltd
Designers: Clare Webber and Simon Borrough
Picture researcher: Rachel Blount
Editors: Sarah Eason and Jennifer Sanderson

Picture credits: Cover: Shutterstock: Rob Crandall (bottom), Romiana Lee (top). Inside:
Shutterstock: Kirstin Adams-Bimson: p. 32; Roman Babakin: p. 18; Brunovalenzano: pp. 5,
44-45; Rob Crandall: pp. 38, 42; Dnetromphotos: p. 9; Everett – Art: p. 21; Everett Historical:
pp. 19, 35; David Gilder: p. 36; Jstone: p. 17; A Katz: p. 33; Karin Hildebrand Lau: p. 12; Niyazz:
p. 31; Sirtravelalot: pp. 14-15t; Wikimedia Commons: pp. 6, 14b; Bill Koplitz: p. 25; Ragesoss:
p. 34; Pete Souza: p. 41; Speaker.gov: p. 11; U.S. Census Bureau: p. 13; U.S. Congress: pp. 27,
28; U.S. Gov: p. 23; White House Photo Office: p. 7.

Cataloging-in-Publication Data

Names: Small, Cathleen.
Title: How does congress work? / Cathleen Small.
Description: New York : Lucent Press, 2019. | Series: American democracy in action |
Includes glossary and index.
Identifiers: ISBN 9781534564022 (pbk.) | ISBN 9781534564008 (library bound)
Subjects: LCSH: United States. Congress--Juvenile literature. | Legislation--United States--
Juvenile literature.
Classification: LCC JK1025.S63 2019 | DDC 328.73--dc23

Printed in the United States of America

CPSIA compliance information: Batch #BS18KL: For further information
contact Greenhaven Publishing LLC, New York, New York, at 1-844-317-7404.

Contents

CHAPTER 1 The Congressional System

The term "congress" can describe any society or organization of people. For example, the National Down Syndrome Congress is an organization dedicated to advocating for the rights of people with Down Syndrome in the United States. The US Sports Congress is a group of high-level executives in the sports industry. The United States Congress is the national legislative (law-making) body in the United States.

What Is the United States Congress?

The U.S. Congress is a group of elected representatives, split into two branches: the Senate and the House of Representatives. The members of both branches meet at the United States Capitol in Washington, D.C.

Congress was established in 1787, when the U.S. Constitution was written. In Article I of the Constitution, the **Framers of the Constitution** wrote, "All legislative Powers herein granted shall be vested in a Congress of the United States, which shall consist of a Senate and a House of Representatives."

The Constitution granted the Senate and the House of Representatives generally equal powers. Both must agree to any new legislation before it is passed into law. In other words, neither branch of Congress holds more or less power than the other.

However, the branches do function somewhat uniquely, in that each has certain duties and powers. The Senate, for example, is the branch that approves appointments to the presidential Cabinet and other federal positions. The Cabinet positions generally get the most public attention. But in reality, somewhere between 1,200 and 1,400 federal positions require confirmation by the Senate.

Senate confirmation of these positions was set forth in Article II of the Constitution, which states, "[The President] shall nominate, and by and with the Advice and Consent of the Senate, shall appoint Ambassadors, other public Ministers and Consuls, Judges of the Supreme Court, and all other Officers of the United States, whose Appointments are not herein otherwise provided for, and which shall be established by Law." In other words, the president can nominate anyone they want to fill these federal positions, but the Senate must confirm these nominations.

The Senate is also in charge of **ratifying** treaties. Treaties are agreements made with other countries, under international law. Peace treaties are just one kind of treaty, but there are many different terms to describe different treaties that countries might enter into, including agreements, protocols, covenants, and conventions. The Paris Accord (also known as the Paris Agreement), which made news in mid-2017 when President Donald Trump withdrew from it, is an example of a treaty.

Congress meets in Washington, D.C., in the United States Capitol building.

Treaties are generally contracts between nations. If a nation fails to meet the terms of the treaty, it can be held liable under international law. According to Article II of the Constitution, "[The President] shall have Power, by and with the Advice and Consent of the Senate, to make Treaties, provided two thirds of the Senators present concur."

The House of Representatives

The House of Representatives, on the other hand, is the branch of Congress that can initiate legislation that will raise revenue, as stated in Article I of the Constitution: "All Bills for raising Revenue shall originate in the House of Representatives; but the Senate may propose or concur with Amendments as on other Bills." In other words, revenue bills start in the House, but the Senate also has a say in them.

The House can start **impeachment** proceedings against a president, though Senate must decide the impeachment. Article I, Section 2, of the Constitution states, "The House of Representatives…shall have the sole Power of Impeachment," granting the power to start impeachment proceedings to the House. However,

The Senate holds impeachment trials.

Article I, Section 3, goes on to state: "The Senate shall have the sole Power to try all Impeachments. When sitting for that Purpose, they shall be on Oath or Affirmation. When the President of the United States is tried, the Chief Justice shall preside: And no Person shall be convicted without the Concurrence of two thirds of the Members present." This means that after the House has started impeachment proceedings, the Senate is the body that makes the decision—and it must be done with a two-thirds majority vote.

According to Article I, Section 3, of the Constitution, "Judgment in Cases of Impeachment shall not extend further than to removal from Office, and disqualification to hold and enjoy any Office of honor, Trust or Profit under the United States: but the Party convicted shall nevertheless be liable and subject to Indictment, Trial, Judgment and Punishment, according to Law." In other words, if the Senate votes to impeach a president, the only consequence given directly by the Senate is that the president is removed from office and banned from holding another office. However, if the president's impeachable offenses broke any sort of law, the impeached president is subject to legal consequences.

It is widely believed that President Richard Nixon was impeached as a result of his cover-up of the Watergate scandal; however, this is untrue. Nixon resigned from office before he could officially be impeached. Presidents Andrew Johnson and Bill Clinton are the only two presidents to have been impeached in the House; however, both were acquitted by the Senate, and neither faced any criminal charges. Impeachment rumors have swirled about President Donald Trump since he took office. They mostly stem from rumors of his involvement in Russian hacking that may have influenced the outcome of the 2016 presidential election. However, by mid-2017, the House had not yet begun impeachment proceedings, and Trump staunchly maintains his innocence.

President Richard Nixon was the thirty-seventh president of the United States. He resigned from office before he could be impeached.

Deciding the President

In the event of a deadlock by the **electoral college** during a presidential election, the House of Representatives can decide the president. This was set forth in the Twelfth Amendment to the Constitution, which states, "If no person have such majority, then from the persons having the highest numbers not exceeding three on the list of those voted for as President, the House of Representatives shall choose immediately, by ballot, the President."

While a deadlocked electoral college seems unlikely in a presidential election, it has happened three times in history. In the 1800 election between candidates Thomas Jefferson and Aaron Burr, the House broke the tie and chose Jefferson as president. The 1800 election prompted the Twelfth Amendment to the Constitution, formally allowing the House to choose the president if no candidate gains a majority of the electoral votes. The House also decided the winner of the 1824 election (John Quincy Adams) when none of the four presidential candidates secured a majority of the electoral votes. And in 1876, the House decided in favor of Rutherford B. Hayes over Samuel J. Tilden when 20 unresolved electoral college votes caused the electoral college to deadlock. The 1876 election was heavily disputed, because ultimately the 20 unresolved electoral votes were given to Hayes as part of the **Compromise of 1877**, despite Tilden having won the **popular vote**.

The House nearly had to decide the presidency in 2000, when George W. Bush narrowly won over Al Gore, with 271 electoral votes to Gore's 266. A candidate needs 270 electoral votes to win. Bush's reelection in 2004 was a narrow win, too. He earned 286 electoral votes over John Kerry's 251. A larger margin than in 2000—but not by much. The largest winning margin in the history of the electoral college was in the 1920 presidential election.

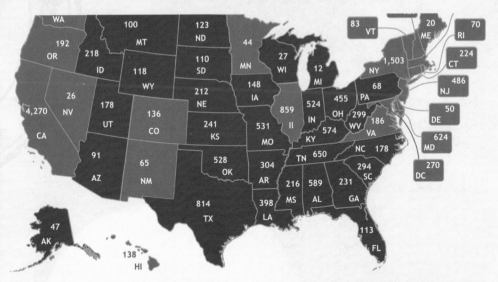

How the United States Voted in 2016

Trump won more states than Clinton in the 2016 election, but Clinton won the vote in many of the most populated states, which won her the popular election overall.

Warren Harding defeated James Cox. Both men were from Ohio, and Republican Harding earned 404 votes compared with Cox's 127.

The Constitution firmly established the two chambers of the legislative branch of government. However, over the years, the two chambers have evolved into the unique groups of elected officials they are today.

HOW WELL DO YOU UNDERSTAND AMERICAN DEMOCRACY?

Technically, a 269–269 vote by the members of the electoral college could happen in any presidential election, resulting in a tie that the House would have to break. If you were writing an amendment to the Constitution, would you grant the tie-breaking power to the House? Or would you create a different system for breaking ties? What might your system look like?

CHAPTER 2

The Two Parts of Congress

The U.S. Congress is considered bicameral, which means it is divided into two chambers. This bicameral structure is a critical part of the country's political structure.

Separation of Powers

A founding principle of the United States is that the government is segmented in a **separation of power**, which upholds democracy and prevents the nation from falling into an **oligarchy** or a **dictatorship**. The three branches of the U.S government are the executive branch (the president), the legislative branch (Congress), and the judicial branch (federal courts and the Supreme Court). Within these three branches, the legislative branch is broken down into the Senate and the House of Representatives, further ensuring separation of power and representation for all citizens.

How the Senate Is Composed

The United States Senate is composed of 2 senators from each of the 50 states, making up a total of 100 members. This was set forth in the Constitution. Article I, Section 3, states, "The Senate of the United States shall be composed of two Senators from each State, chosen by the Legislature thereof, for six Years; and each Senator shall have one Vote." When the Constitution was written, there were not yet 50 states. However, the Framers of the Constitution wrote it in such a way that the total number of states is irrelevant. Each state will have two senators, regardless of how many states there are in the nation.

This photograph shows the 114th Congress of the United States. A total of 471 members were elected or reelected on November 4, 2014. The 114th Congress convened, or assembled, on January 3, 2015. It concluded, or dissolved, on January 3, 2017.

The Framers of the Constitution wrote "chosen by the Legislature thereof," meaning that senators were to be chosen by each state's legislature. That has since changed. In the mid-1850s, there were often vacant Senate seats. The process of choosing senators had been left up to the states, so when they had internal disputes, it sometimes resulted in them being unable to choose a senator.

It also became apparent that not all methods for choosing senators were consistent. This led to disputes about the validity of some senators' appointments. Bribery and intimidation were reportedly factors in some states, and the Senate saw nine bribery cases between 1866 and 1906 with regard to election of senators.

In 1826, **direct election** of senators was proposed, but the Senate was resistant to the change. A petition for a popular election for senators was sent to the House of Representatives in the 1870s, but the process remained as it had been.

There was growing frustration with the process, and in the early 1900s, Oregon took matters into its own hands and began developing a direct election system, which it fully implemented in 1907. Nebraska soon followed suit. Within 5 years, 29 states were moving toward a direct election system for senators, and the Seventeenth Amendment to the Constitution was passed.

The Seventeenth Amendment states, "The Senate of the United States shall be composed of two Senators from each State, elected by the people thereof, for six years." In other words, "chosen by the Legislature thereof" was changed to "elected by the people thereof." And ever since, senators have been elected by the **constituents** of their state.

Voters turned out for a rally at the University of Montana in 2017. They were showing their support for House of Representatives candidate Rob Quist.

HOW WELL DO YOU UNDERSTAND AMERICAN DEMOCRACY?

While the change to a popular vote for U.S. senators is generally considered a positive move, there is still the danger that this type of vote can lead to a popularity contest. A particularly charismatic or shrewd candidate could become elected by winning over the majority of citizens, even if that candidate is not necessarily the best fit for office. What measures might you take to try to avoid that outcome, if you were drafting a further amendment to the Constitution?

How the House of Representatives Is Composed

Unlike the Senate, which simply has two senators from each state, the makeup of the House of Representatives depends on the number of people in each state. The United States census, which is held every ten years, determines the population for each state and region, and this information is used to determine **congressional districts**. Each congressional district has one representative in the House of Representatives.

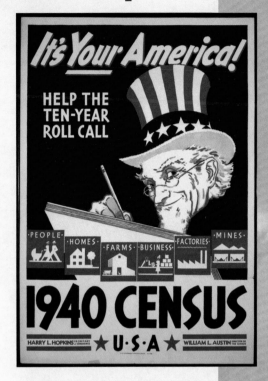

The United States census is used to determine congressional districts.

The total number of members of the House of Representatives is 435. However, this was not always the case. In Article I, Section 2, of the original Constitution, the Framers of the Constitution stated, "Representatives and direct Taxes shall be apportioned among the several States which may be included within this Union, according to their respective Numbers, which shall be determined by adding to the whole Number of free Persons, including those bound to Service for a Term of Years, and excluding Indians not taxed, three fifths of all other Persons. The actual Enumeration shall be made within three Years after the first Meeting of the Congress of the United States, and within every subsequent Term of ten Years, in such Manner as they shall by Law direct. The Number of Representatives shall not exceed one for every thirty Thousand, but each State shall have at Least one Representative."

Obviously, the reference to "free Persons" is no longer valid, given that slavery has long since been outlawed in the United States, and all U.S. citizens are free people. Representatives may now represent far more than 30,000 people.

However, the general idea is still the same. The Apportionment Act of 1911 established the fixed number of representatives at 435. The Reapportionment Act of 1929 upheld the establishment of 435 representatives, but set forth further regulations about how districts were allocated. States with greater population density have great numbers of representatives, while less-densely populated states have fewer representatives. Currently, California has the greatest number of representatives in the House, with 53. Seven states have only one representative: Delaware, Vermont, North Dakota, South Dakota, Wyoming, Alaska, and Montana. All seven of these states have low population density. Alaska is actually the largest state geographically and Montana is the fourth-largest state, but these two states are just particularly low in population density.

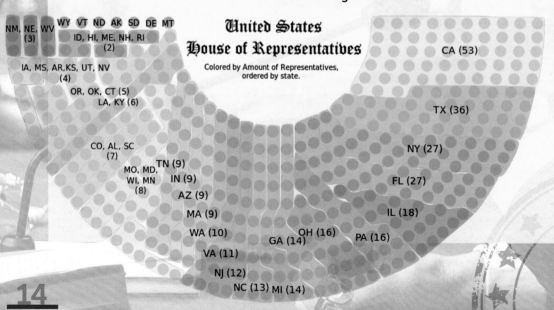

Representatives in the House are assigned seats according to their state.

United States
House of Representatives
Colored by Amount of Representatives, ordered by state.

NM, NE, WV (3)
WY VT ND AK SD DE MT
ID, HI, ME, NH, RI (2)
IA, MS, AR, KS, UT, NV (4)
OR, OK, CT (5)
LA, KY (6)
CO, AL, SC (7)
MO, MD, WI, MN (8)
TN (9)
IN (9)
AZ (9)
MA (9)
WA (10)
VA (11)
NJ (12)
NC (13)
MI (14)
GA (14)
OH (16)
PA (16)
IL (18)
FL (27)
NY (27)
TX (36)
CA (53)

NONVOTING MEMBERS OF CONGRESS

In addition to the elected officials in the Senate and the House of Representatives, six nonvoting delegates are included in the House of Representatives. These delegates are from U.S. districts or territories, which are not considered states, though they generally operate under U.S. law. These territories and districts include Washington, D.C., American Samoa, Guam, the Northern Mariana Islands, Puerto Rico, and the U.S. Virgin Islands.

Nonvoting delegates in the House cannot vote on proposed legislation that goes in front of the full House. However, they can vote in certain committees, such as the Committee of the Whole, which is essentially made up of all members of the House. Whether their vote actually counts in the Committee of the Whole is questionable. The rules on that keep changing back and forth, depending on which political party is in control of Congress and how it thinks nonvoting delegates' votes might affect voting outcomes. Even though nonvoting delegates generally cannot vote, they are however, allowed to introduce legislation.

Like other members of the House of Representatives, most nonvoting delegates are elected every two years. However, the resident commissioner, who is the nonvoting delegate from Puerto Rico, is elected every four years.

Members of the House represent the people of the United States.

CHAPTER 3

How Office Is Held

Although the requirements are similar for becoming a senator or a member of the House of Representatives, the terms of office differ between the two.

Eligibility for the Senate

According to Article I, Section 3, of the Constitution, "No Person shall be a Senator who shall not have attained to the Age of thirty Years, and been nine Years a Citizen of the United States, and who shall not, when elected, be an Inhabitant of that State for which he shall be chosen." This means that senators must be at least 30 years old, must have been a U.S. citizen for at least 9 years, and must officially live in the state for which they will be senator.

Sometimes, a politician with an eye on a Senate seat will move to a particular state and establish residency so they can run for an open seat. Hillary Clinton did so in 2000. She was born and raised in Illinois, lived for years in Arkansas (where her husband was governor) after graduating college (in Massachusetts) and law school (in Connecticut), then lived for eight years in Washington, D.C. (while her husband was president). She finally moved to New York in 2000. New Yorkers were suspicious at first: they wondered how well Clinton would represent them when she was not really a New Yorker, born and bred. Ultimately, she won over many, and she has lived in New York for almost two decades now. Clinton is far from the first person to adopt a new state as their home in an effort to run for Senate.

Hillary Clinton established residency in New York so that she could run for the U.S. Senate in that state.

Massachusetts-raised Bobby Kennedy Jr., brother of President John F. Kennedy, did the same thing in the 1960s.

When the Framers of the Constitution considered how to word Article I, Section 3, they considered whether to include religious and property requirements in the Constitution. That is, should they add that candidates must practice a particular religion or own property? Ultimately, they voted against these two criteria.

Much of the Constitution was inspired by a precedent set by British government. Although citizens of the United States no longer wanted to live under the British Crown, they could not deny that much of the precedent set forth under the British government was sound, and so that inspired parts of the Constitution.

One such part is the citizenship portion of Article I, Section 3. English law stated that no member of either House of Parliament could be born outside of England, Scotland, or Ireland. The Framers found this to be a bit too strict but decided that members of Congress should have a certain amount of time as United States citizens before being allowed to take office.

The Framers also considered state residency laws when determining the amount of time one must be a U.S. citizen before taking office. Different states had different residency requirements before a citizen could hold a state office. New Hampshire, for example, required people to be residents for seven years before being eligible for state office. Other states set requirements at one, three, or five years.

The Framers worried that an outright ban would be discouraging to potential immigrants, many of whom had supported the United States in the Revolutionary War. On the other hand, they worried that having too-short residency requirements might produce senators who could not set aside their loyalty to their home country when negotiating matters of international relations, such as treaties. Ultimately, the Framers settled on nine years as an appropriate length of time for a citizenship requirement. To them, it seemed to be a good compromise between an outright ban of foreign-born citizens being eligible for office, and potentially allowing people to hold office who might still be under the influence of their home country.

The Rayburn House Office Building holds the offices for more than 100 members of the House of Representatives.

Eligibility for the House of Representatives

Article I, Section 2, of the Constitution states, "No Person shall be a Representative who shall not have attained to the age of twenty five Years, and been seven Years a Citizen of the United States, and who shall not, when elected, be an Inhabitant of that State in which he shall be chosen." This means that members of the House must be at least 25 years old, must have been a U.S. citizen for at least 7 years, and must reside in the state for which they are pursuing a seat.

It might seem odd that the age requirement for a member of the House is lower than that of the Senate. However, James Madison explained the reasoning in *The Federalist*, No. 62. Madison stated that because Senate duties include deliberation on important matters, senators needed to have a more stable character and a greater knowledge base than members of the House. It is said that wisdom comes with age, and it seems Madison and the Framers felt that five additional years could bring added wisdom to senators.

Originally, the minimum age proposed for members of the House of Representatives was 21. However, George Mason (one of the Framers from Virginia) proposed that the minimum age be changed to 25 because citizens were officially adults at 21, and Mason felt they should have a period of time to learn how to manage their own affairs before they took a position in which they would be managing the affairs of the nation. Once again, with age would come wisdom.

George Mason was one of the Framers of the Constitution.

Similarly, the citizenship requirements are shorter for members of the House than for senators. Members of the House need only be citizens of the United States for seven years before being eligible for election.

One reason why the qualifications were a bit more lax for members of the House was that the Framers wanted the House to be the part of the legislative branch of government closest to the people. The office of the president was a hallowed office, held far separate from citizens. United States senators were a step below: still typically not accessible to the public, but more approachable than the president. The members of the House, on the other hand, were frequently elected (serving two-year terms) and were considered much closer to the citizens they represented.

Both senators and representatives were bound by the same terms in Article VI of the Constitution: "The Senators and Representatives before mentioned, and the Members of the several State Legislatures, and all executive and judicial Officers, both of the United States and of the several States, shall be bound by Oath or Affirmation, to support this Constitution; but no religious Test shall ever be required as a Qualification to any Office or public Trust under the United States." In other words, all members of Congress (as well as executive and judicial officers and members of state legislatures) were bound to uphold the Constitution—but they could be assured that their religion would never be a factor.

The mention of religion was important, and James Madison noted it in *The Federalist*, No. 52. Madison stated that Congress was open to candidates of any country of birth, financial status, profession, or religious faith. Many who had come to North America were fleeing religious **persecution** in their home countries (even England, where the Church of England was often at odds with the Catholic Church), and it was important to the Framers that religious freedom be preserved in the United States for all—including members of Congress.

The Election Process for Members of Congress

Both members of the House and senators are elected by direct, popular election, though that was not always the case. Senators used to be chosen by their state legislature, but that process ended with the ratification of the Seventeenth Amendment in 1912.

Senators serve a term of six years. Members of the House serve two-year terms, ending on even years. The entire body of U.S. senators is not up for election every six years, though. Every two years, an election is held in which one-third of U.S. Senate seats are up for reelection. That way, on any given election year, two-thirds of the Senate will remain the same, with only one-third of the seats turning over.

In *The Federalist*, James Madison explained explained why certain clauses were written into the Constitution.

THE PROCESS FOR VACANCIES

In addition to changing the manner in which senators are elected, the Seventeenth Amendment also set forth rules about how vacancies in Senate seats would be handled. The Amendment states, "When vacancies happen in the representation of any State in the Senate, the executive authority of such State shall issue writs of election to fill such vacancies: Provided, That the legislature of any State may empower the executive thereof to make temporary appointments until the people fill the vacancies by election as the legislature may direct." In other words, if a Senate seat becomes vacant for any reason, the governor can appoint a temporary senator to serve until a special election is held to fill the seat.

The process is a bit different in the House of Representatives. According to Article I, Section 2, of the Constitution, "When vacancies happen in the Representation from any State, the Executive Authority thereof shall issue Writs of Election to fill such Vacancies." This means that a newly elected member must fill vacant seats in the House. If Congress is in its first session of the term, the seat will be filled by a special election. However, if the vacancy occurs during the second session of Congress, the seat may be filled by special election, or it may simply be filled during the next general election. The House can still run if there are vacant seats, though if the number of vacant seats is greater than 100, state governments will normally hold special elections to fill seats, even if Congress is in its second session.

Both senators and members of the House can serve as many terms as they wish, if their constituents reelect them. Unlike the office of the president, there are no **term limits** for members of Congress. The longest-serving senator thus far was Robert C. Byrd, a Democrat from West Virginia who served from 1959 until his death in 2010. The longest-serving member of the House of Representatives was John Dingell, a Democrat from Michigan who served from 1955 until his retirement in 2015. The shortest-serving member of Congress was Effingham Lawrence, who served just one day in Congress in 1875. Lawrence had actually lost the election in 1872 to his opponent, but courts voided his opponent's win and gave the seat to Lawrence—the day before the last day of the Congressional session.

Senator Robert Byrd takes the oath of office for his ninth term. He is the longest-serving member of the Senate.

HOW WELL DO YOU UNDERSTAND AMERICAN DEMOCRACY?

Some people have argued that there should be term limits for members of Congress, as there are for presidents. Do you agree or disagree? What points would you make in your argument for or against term limits for members of Congress?

CHAPTER 4

The Structure of Congress

Congress is composed of 535 members—100 senators and 435 members of the House of Representatives. Within Congress, there are numerous divisions in committees, task forces, and the like. There are also officers who take a lead role in each branch of Congress.

Congressional Committees

Congressional committees handle duties that are more specialized than the general duties of Congress. They focus on much more specific areas. The number of issues coming before Congress is vast: there are legislative matters dealing with crime, punishment, health care, immigration, finance, civil rights, international relations and policy, and the list goes on and on. Members participate in committees so they can focus their efforts on more specific areas and become, as much as possible, "experts" in policy in those areas.

While the number of committees fluctuates, there are roughly 200 committees and subcommittees in Congress. Each committee gathers information about topics in its area of focus, evaluates possible legislation in these areas, identifies policy problems, proposes solutions where needed, monitors action by the executive branch of the government in these areas, investigates any allegations of wrongdoing, and determines what issues should be brought to the floor in front of the entire Congress. There are several types of committees, including standing committees, select or special committees, and joint committees.

The **Appropriations** Committee holds a hearing in Washington, D.C.
The Appropriations Committee is the largest committee in the Senate.

Standing Committees

Standing committees were established in 1816. They consider bills and recommend issues for consideration by the House and Senate. They also monitor programs, activities, and agencies in their area of expertise. They recommend funding levels for new and existing programs, as well as for government operations.

These committees have anywhere from 6 to 50 members. In the House of Representatives, members can serve on no more than two standing committees and four subcommittees at a time. However, this rule may be waived in certain circumstances. In the Senate, members can serve on up to three full committees and up to five subcommittees at once.

There are 16 standing committees in the Senate and 20 in the House. Most committees are divided into subcommittees, though the Budget Committee, Ethics Committee, and the House Administration Committee have no subdivisions. Most Senate committees are also divided into subcommittees. In both the House and Senate, each committee or subcommittee has a chair and a ranking member.

Select Committees

Select or special committees actually began even earlier than standing committees—in 1789, during the first session of Congress. At that time, select committees were formed to perform special functions in Congress, and they were dissolved as soon as the task was complete. The first committee, in 1789, lasted just five days. Its task was to prepare rules and orders for the House proceedings. In current Congress, select committees can be temporary or permanent. Most are temporary, but some, such as the Senate Select Committee on Intelligence, are permanent.

Select committees are usually formed to examine issues that do not quite fit into standing committees, or that may apply to multiple standing committees. Select committees sometimes consider measures, and they sometimes conduct studies or investigations. In general, select committees are more investigative than standing committees. Standing committees can draft legislation, whereas select committees generally do the investigation behind issues.

On rare occasions, select committees have become standing committees. One example is the Ways and Means Committee, which oversees issues related to taxation, **tariffs**, and raising revenue. It was established as a select committee in 1789 and existed for only two months. However, by 1801, it had become a standing committee that is still in effect today.

Joint Committees

Joint committees are so named because they are composed of members from both the House and Senate. Joint committees do not generally consider measures—they attend to housekeeping tasks and sometimes perform studies on a given issue.

Joint committees are usually permanent, though sometimes temporary joint committees are formed when the House and Senate cannot agree on a particular measure. These temporary joint committees are called conference committees. They draft compromises on a measure that will theoretically be agreeable to both the House of Representatives and the Senate.

Officers in Congress

While each person in Congress has one vote (except for nonvoting delegates) and thus is essentially equal, there are certain officers that serve in Congress. In the House of Representatives, the presiding officer is the Speaker of the House, who also happens to be second in line for the presidency, behind the vice president.

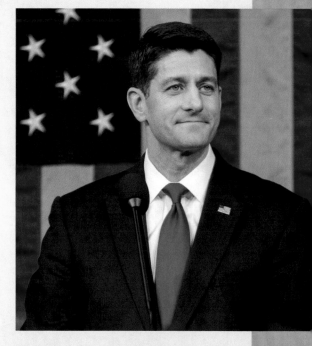

Paul Ryan is Speaker of the House under President Donald Trump.

In the Senate, the presiding officer is technically the vice president of the United States, who also serves as the president of the Senate. However, the vice president is often absent (performing duties as vice president of the United States), so the Senate also chooses a president pro tempore to act in the vice president's absence. Both the Speaker of the House and the president pro tempore are members of the political party that holds power in their respective chamber of Congress. That is, if the Senate is controlled by a Republican majority, the president pro tempore will be a Republican. If a Democratic majority controls the House, the Speaker of the House will be a Democrat.

SPEAKER OF THE HOUSE NANCY PELOSI: BREAKING THE GENDER BARRIER

When Congress was first established, it was understood that all members would be white men. That has long since changed; however, men still typically hold the power positions in Congress. Nancy Pelosi, a congresswoman representing California's twelfth district, broke barriers when she became the first female Speaker of the House in 2007. Pelosi served in the office until 2011. By early 2018, she was still the only woman to ever hold the position. She is still an active congresswoman and is the House Minority Leader, representing the Democratic Party. She has been a member of the House since 1993.

Nancy Pelosi is the first woman, first Californian, and first Italian-American to lead a major party in Congress.

Other leaders in the House of Representatives that are elected by their respective parties include the Majority Leader (who is the head of the party currently in power in the House), the Minority Leader (the head of the party not currently in power in the House), the Minority and Majority Whips, and the assistant party leaders.

Whips have the difficult task of keeping order in the House. They invite members of the House to vote, and encourage them to vote along party lines. They also keep track of the votes on a particular piece of legislation. If a piece of legislation is going to easily pass with a majority, then the whip's job is fairly easy—they just count the votes. If the vote is close, the whip gets to "whip up" support for their party's position.

In addition to the president and president pro tempore, the Senate has party secretaries for both the majority and minority parties, as well as an overall secretary of the Senate. Like the House, each party in the Senate also has a leader and a whip.

Members of each political party in Congress also select floor leaders and other officials. In the Senate, elected officers include the Chaplain, Chief Administrative Officer, Clerk of the House, and Sergeant at Arms. Appointed officials in the House are the General Counsel, Historian, Inspector General, and Parliamentarian.

CHAPTER 5

The Powers of Congress

Although the president is the figurehead of the United States government, Congress is actually more powerful than the president in some ways. This is partly a result of the system of checks and balances that the Framers of the Constitution created to ensure that complete power did not fall into the hands of one individual or a small group of individuals.

Checks and Balances

The three branches of the United States government all function both independently and together. The legislative branch, composed of the two chambers of Congress, generally makes the laws that govern the country. This is, in some ways, an independent process. Senators and members of the House propose legislation, gather support, and ultimately vote whether to pass it. However, the process is also linked to the two other branches of government. The executive branch must approve the legislation for it to be passed into law. If the executive branch (the president) decides instead to **veto** the legislation, then Congress can vote on whether to override the veto or accept it.

The judicial branch steps in when legislation is signed by the president and passed into law, but then comes under challenge through the lower courts. For example, in 2017, federal legislation called the Individuals with Disabilities Education Act (IDEA) was called into question. The main goal of IDEA is to protect the rights of students with disabilities in the education system.

The three branches of government provide a system of checks and balances that ensures no one branch holds too much power.

One family in Colorado felt that its school district was not upholding IDEA, so they took the school district to court. The family lost, but appealed to a higher court. The case continued moving up through the judicial system and ultimately found its way to the Supreme Court in 2017. *Endrew F. v. Douglas County School District* was settled by a landmark 8-0 Supreme Court decision, which overturned the lower courts' rulings and stated that the school district had indeed failed the student in question. This ruling opens the possibility to future revisions that will strengthen IDEA and make it better serve the needs of students with disabilities.

While the Supreme Court's unanimous ruling in *Endrew F. v. Douglas County School District* was unusual because it is rare for all eight justices (**conservative** and **liberal**) to agree unanimously, having the Supreme Court or other federal courts make decisions that change law is not all that unusual. The Endrew case was noteworthy because it involved a population (disabled students) that is typically **marginalized,** and because the decision was unanimous. However, new and revised interpretation of laws based on federal or Supreme Court decisions is fairly common. In this manner, the judicial branch keeps a check on the legislative branch.

The judicial branch can also keep a check on the executive branch. For example, in 2017, President Trump attempted to enact a "travel ban" in which people from seven predominantly Muslim countries would be temporarily banned from entering the United States. The federal courts rapidly halted his executive order.

In turn, the executive branch and the legislative branch keep a check on the judicial branch. Justices to the Supreme Court are nominated by the president and confirmed by the Senate.

This complex system of checks and balances has many pieces and some **loopholes**, but in general it works to keep one branch of the government from becoming too powerful, and it keeps total power over the country from falling into the hands of a small group of people.

HOW WELL DO YOU UNDERSTAND AMERICAN DEMOCRACY?

While the system of checks and balances works reasonably well between the three branches of government, it is not a foolproof system. Where do you see holes that could potentially allow one branch of the government to have perhaps more power than is appropriate? What would you do to try to plug that hole?

Protestors in Sacramento, California, demonstrated against President Trump's "travel ban."

STANDING
SLAMOPHOBIA
& RACISM

NOPE
NOPE

IMMIGRANTS
ARE NOT
CRIMINALS!
ANSWERcoalition.org

Powers of the Senate

The Senate has many powers, some of which overlap that of the House of Representatives, and others which do not. Both chambers have the authority to propose and vote on legislation. However, the Senate has some specific powers that the House does not have. One example is the power to conduct impeachment hearings. While the House is the chamber that calls for impeachment, the Senate is the chamber that actually holds the impeachment trial and ultimately votes whether to impeach a president or other federal official.

The Senate also has the power to approve or reject presidential nominations of various officials in the Cabinet and the federal government. Often, the Senate ends up approving presidential nominees, but sometimes it is not a sure thing. For example, in 2017, the Senate very nearly rejected President Donald Trump's nominee for Secretary of Education, Betsy DeVos. Many found her unsuitable for the job and were concerned about her agenda for the future of public education in the United States. The Senate confirmation hearings for DeVos were tense and drama-filled. The vote ended in a tie, which had to be broken by the President of the Senate and Vice President of the United States, Mike Pence.

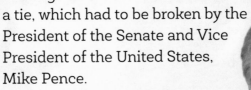

President Trump's nomination of Betsy DeVos for Secretary of Education was met with criticism and concern over her proposed policies.

The Senate also has power over the process of approving treaties. Treaties made in the executive branch of the government must be approved by a two-thirds Senate vote. The Senate also has the power to amend treaties. In general, the Senate usually approves treaties made by the president, but they have occasionally rejected them. For example, in 2012, the Senate rejected a United Nations treaty aimed at banning discrimination against people with disabilities, backed by President Obama. While the ultimate goal was a positive one, senators who voted against the treaty were concerned that would open up new abortion rights and limit the ability of citizens to homeschool their disabled children.

The Senate has the power to expel members for disorderly conduct—a power that the House also has. It is not something that happens often, but since 1789, the Senate has expelled 15 people. If the Senate feels that a member should be disciplined for disorderly conduct, but not necessarily expelled, they can also make a formal statement of disapproval called a censure. The Senate has exercised this right nine times since 1789. The House also has this power of censure.

The Senate also has the power to **filibuster** if it wants to delay a vote or stop legislation from going through. A filibuster is a long speech that holds the Senate floor so that no vote can be held. On a similar note, the Senate has the power of **cloture** as well—they can end a debate with a three-fifths majority vote.

Until recently, Senator Chris Murphy from Connecticut was the youngest member of the Senate.

THE FILIBUSTER TO END ALL FILIBUSTERS

South Carolina Senator Strom Thurmond famously held the longest filibuster in history in August 1957, when he spoke for 24 hours and 18 minutes to try to block the passage of the Civil Rights Act of 1957. A filibuster does not necessarily need to be strictly focused on the topic at hand. When Thurmond filibustered in 1957, he spent some of his time on the floor reciting the Declaration of Independence, the Bill of Rights, various other historical documents, and the farewell address of President George Washington. A filibuster is simply a delay tactic, and the requirement is that the person filibustering must not give up the floor—even if they are simply talking about something unrelated.

Thurmond was not alone in filibustering against the Civil Rights Act of 1957. In a three-month span in 1957, various senators spent a combined total of 57 days filibustering to delay the vote on the Civil Rights Act. Other remarkably long filibusters have taken place on issues ranging from military spending to U.S. Treasury lending.

Robert B. Elliott delivers an impassioned speech in the House of Representatives supporting the 1874 Civil Rights Act.

If investigation is needed in relation to the executive branch of government, the Senate has the power to conduct investigations. For example, in 2017, the Senate launched an investigation into President Trump's alleged involvement in the rumored Russian hacking of the 2016 presidential election.

Both the House and the Senate also have the power to judge the qualifications of their respective members. If there is a contested election of a member into Congress, the chamber involved has the power to settle it.

Rob Quist ran for Congress in a 2017 special election, but he narrowly lost to his opponent Greg Gianforte.

Powers of the House of Representatives

The Senate holds certain powers, and so does the House of Representatives. As mentioned earlier, the House has the power to set the impeachment process in motion if its members feel the president or another federal official has committed an impeachable offense.

The House also has the power to elect the president of the United States if there is a tie in the electoral college. In general, the House of Representatives is thought to represent the interests of the people of the United States, whereas the Senate is thought to represent the interests of each state. So, with that in mind, it makes sense that the House would be the chamber with the power to elect the president if there is a tie in the electoral college.

The House of Representatives also has the power to introduce legislation dealing with taxes and revenue. In fact, Article I, Section 7, of the U.S. Constitution states that "all bills for raising revenue shall originate in the House of Representatives." Often, the president makes a recommendation for new tax legislation, then the House Ways and Means Committee initiates the legislation. Only when the legislation has been approved in the House of Representatives does it then go to the Senate to work its way through the approval process in that chamber.

The House of Representatives can also introduce other types of legislation, but so can the Senate—it is only revenue-raising legislation that must first start in the House.

Both the House of Representatives and the Senate have the power to have members participate in joint committees with other members from both chambers. And together, the House and Senate hold the power to declare war.

CHAPTER 6

Congressional Procedures

Congress runs reasonably smoothly because of a long-established set of procedures that guides legislation through the process. Without the procedures put in place, congressional debate could, in theory, turn into nothing more than an arguing match. While the procedure for passing new legislation is rather complex, it generally results in a carefully examined, and often significantly amended, bill becoming law.

Congressional Sessions

At the most basic level, Congress is divided into sessions. There is one term for each year. Members of the House of Representatives serve two-year terms, so each term is made up of two sessions of Congress, which generally begin on or near January 3.

Congress comes together in a joint session for events such as the State of the Union address.

The meetings held during a congressional session must take place at the United States Capitol. Neither chamber of Congress can adjourn, or take a recess, for more than three days unless the other chamber has also agreed to do so.

Sometimes, a joint session of Congress will be held if there is a situation that requires a concurrent resolution in both chambers of Congress. One such example of a joint session occurs when the electoral votes are counted for a presidential election. Usually, the Speaker of the House presides over joint sessions. However, in the case of the count of electoral college votes, the president of the Senate presides over the joint session instead.

Introducing and Passing Legislation

Anyone can have an idea for new legislation. However, for that legislation to actually be passed into law, a specific procedure must be followed.

First, a member of Congress must introduce a bill. If someone who is not a member of Congress has an idea for a bill, that person must find a member of Congress to sponsor the bill. A bill can be sponsored by just one member of Congress, or it can have many co-sponsors. That member or those members will then officially introduce the bill by placing it in the **hopper** on the clerk's desk (if the bill is introduced in the House of Representatives), or by placing it on the presiding officer's desk (if it is introduced in the Senate). The clerk will then assign the bill a number and pass it to the appropriate committee.

The committee will carefully study the bill and may make changes to it. Sometimes, the committee will revise it significantly and introduce an entirely new bill. Other times, the committee will decide to **table** the bill, essentially killing it.

The bill may then be given to the appropriate subcommittee for further review. Sometimes, it is simply reported back to the floor of the chamber of Congress, but often it goes to subcommittee review. The subcommittee goes through a similar process of review and revision.

Once the bill has been released from the committee or subcommittee, a report of the bill is ordered, and the bill is then sent to the floor for consideration. On the floor, members of the House or Senate will debate the bill. The bill will be read, debated, potentially amended, reread, debated some more, potentially amended again, then read again and debated one final time, with perhaps final amendments made. Then, and only then, the bill will be put up for a vote.

If the bill passes the vote, it will then be sent to the other chamber of Congress and will undergo a similar process there.

THE FORMS OF PROPOSALS FOR NEW LEGISLATION

Proposed new legislation can take one of four forms. The first is a bill, which can be introduced in either the House or the Senate. Bills introduced in the House are given a number starting with H.R., and bills introduced in the Senate are given a number starting with S. Joint resolutions are very similar to bills and are treated the same—they are usually used when the matter concerns continuing or emergency appropriations. Concurrent resolutions affect the House and Senate only, so they do not need presidential approval. Simple resolutions affect either the House or the Senate only, and also do not need presidential approval.

When the bill has passed in both chambers of Congress, it is sent to the president. If the president signs the bill, it becomes law. If the president takes no action within 10 days, the bill automatically is passed into law. If the president vetoes the bill, then the Senate will decide whether to attempt to overturn the president's veto with a two-thirds vote.

President Barack Obama reacted by applauding when the Affordable Care Act was passed in 2010.

HOW WELL DO YOU UNDERSTAND AMERICAN DEMOCRACY?

In 2017, health care was a hotly debated subject in Congress. The House passed a health care bill that many felt would be devastating to a large portion of Americans. The Senate then began work on its version of the bill, which many felt was even worse than the House bill. Congress attempted to fast-track a vote on the bill but was forced to suspend the Senate vote when it became clear it did not have enough Senate support to pass the bill. What measures would you put in place to ensure that a potentially harmful bill could not be fast-tracked through Congress?

The Complex Structure of Congress

There is no doubt that the structure of Congress and how it functions is complex. However, there is no simple way to run a country of more than 322 million citizens. The bicameral structure of Congress works well to ensure that the interests of both individual citizens and collective states are supported.

The separation of power between the executive branch, the judicial branch, and Congress (the legislative branch) also serves to protect the interests of American citizens. In nations that do not have some type of separation of power, there is a very real danger of a small group of individuals gaining control over the country.

Senators generally represent the interests of the states they are from, while members of the House of Representatives support the interests of the citizens of their district.

It is nearly impossible for a small group of people to truly have everyone's best interests at heart. Even people who try to bring an objective viewpoint to issues have bias, and sometimes bias can negatively impact a group, or groups, of citizens.

For example, consider the hotly debated topic of gun control and Second Amendment rights—the right to bear arms. Usually, Democrats tend to favor stricter gun control laws, while Republicans tend to favor less government intervention and more rights for citizens to bear arms. Without the two-party system that exists in the United States, one group of the population would lose in this debate: If the country were solely Republican-controlled, citizens who are in favor of stricter gun control laws would feel unsafe. If the country were controlled solely by Democrats, citizens who value their ability to own firearms would feel as though their rights were being taken away.

The fact that Congress is made up of a two-party system helps lessen this problem. The idea is that although one party will always control Congress (whichever one has the majority), the citizens who share the other party's viewpoints will be still be represented. Congress being composed of two chambers helps, too. If only the Senate existed, it would be much more likely for either Democrats or Republicans to gain an extremely strong majority. After all, there are only two senators to elect from each state. However, the House is composed of so many representatives that it helps balance this out. The House helps ensure that both parties and their citizens will be represented.

It may seem as though there would be simpler ways to structure a government. But, in reality, the structure of Congress is part of what keeps everyone's voice heard and represented in the United States government.

Passing a Bill in Action

- **Bill is introduced by member of House or Senate**

- **Bill's first reading**

- **Bill is referred to House or Senate committee**

- **Committee reviews bill, then returns it to member of House or Senate**

- **Bill's second reading**

- **Debate on bill and first vote**

- **Bill's third reading, final debate, and vote**

- **If passed, the bill is sent to the second chamber where the process repeats**

- **If House and Senate bills differ, bill goes to conference committee**

- **If passed, the bill may be signed into law or vetoed by the president**

Glossary

appropriations Assets distributed for a special purpose.

cloture A procedure to end debate and call a vote.

Compromise of 1877 An agreement that settled the 1876 presidential election and resulted in the government removing troops from the South, thus ending the Reconstruction Era after the Civil War.

congressional districts Regions of roughly 700,000 electors that elect a single representative to the House of Representatives.

conservative Describes one who values traditional systems and is cautious about new innovation.

constituents Voting members of a community.

dictatorship A country ruled by a person who has total power that was usually gained by force.

direct election An election in which voters directly select their preferred candidate for office.

electoral college The body of official voters, representing each state, who formally cast the votes for president of the United States.

filibuster An action that stalls progress in a legislative assembly.

Framers of the Constitution The delegates who went to the Constitutional Convention and ultimately drafted the Constitution.

hopper The box in which bills are placed for consideration by the legislature.

impeachment Charges of misconduct against a person who holds a high public office.

liberal One who is open to new ideas and innovation and is willing to change traditional systems.

loopholes Small mistakes in agreements that give someone ways or opportunities to avoid having to do something.

marginalized Treated as insignificant and/or discriminated against.

oligarchy A country ruled by a small group of people.

persecution Hostility and discrimination based on religion, political beliefs, race, or other factors.

popular vote A simple form of election in which the candidate with the most votes wins.

ratifying Giving formal consent to a new law, treaty, contract, or agreement, thus making it valid.

separation of power The principle that power is divided among the three branches of government.

table To postpone the consideration of an issue.

tariffs Taxes or fees to be paid on imports or exports.

term limits Limits on the number of terms that an official can hold a particular elected office.

veto To reject a proposed law.

For More Information

Books

Committee on House Administration of the U.S. House of Representatives. *Women in the United States Congress: 1917–2014*. North Charleston, SC: CreateSpace Independent Publishing Platform, 2015.

Ethridge, Emily. *Powerful Women: The 25 Most Influential Women in Congress*. Washington, D.C.: CQ Roll Call, 2015.

McAuliffe, Bill. *The U.S. House of Representatives* (By the People). Mankato, MN: Creative Education, 2017.

McAuliffe, Bill. *The U.S. Senate* (By the People). Mankato, MN: Creative Education, 2017.

Websites

Readers interested in someday doing an internship with the House of Representatives will find helpful information at:
www.house.gov/content/educate/internships.php

To watch live proceedings of the Senate, log on at:
www.senate.gov/floor

The official website for the House of Representatives contains the latest happenings in the House, and links to historical and reference information. To watch live proceedings of the House of Representatives, log on at:
www.house.gov

The official website for the United States Senate has helpful links to history of the Senate, and reference materials about this chamber of Congress:
www.senate.gov

Publisher's note to educators and parents: Our editors have carefully reviewed these websites to ensure that they are suitable for students. Many websites change frequently, however, and we cannot guarantee that a site's future contents will continue to meet our high standards of quality and educational value. Be advised that students should be closely supervised whenever they access the Internet.

Index